THE WILLING SLAVE

Written by Kingsley Onwu

Published by New Generation Publishing in 2018

First Edition

www.newgeneration-publishing.com

New Generation Publishing

I like to dedicate this book to the families of William Wilberforce; Thomas Clarkson To all white British and white Americans, people of other races who have been supporting, lending their voices and resourses for equality. And to all who laid down their lives for the freedom of the black race, the Abraham Lincolns of this world. To my ever loving dad Christian Onwu who passed on while I was writing this book. To my family for all their love and support

THE AGONY OF A MOTHER

Who will comfort me?
Who will comfort me?
Who will wipe these tears away from my eyes?
How can I forget the pain I felt in my heart?
As my beloved husband and sons were forcefully snatched away from me
and carried into captivity, to an unknown land through the high sea?
Oh, who will comfort me?
I became desolate.
My joy, pride and happiness were gone.
But I never seized praying on my knees
that God will one day bring my husband and sons back to me,
to comfort me, wipe away my tears and rebuild their land that now lie in waste.
My pain was made worse by the news
that my beloved, strong and able-bodied husband has died in exile,
in the hands of the slave masters who made him,
and my sons work as slaves in their farms and plantations.
Beaten, dehumanized and tortured. Tortured to death.
Who will comfort me?
Now my knees are hurting, hurting from ceaseless prayers.
My faith almost gone, hmmmm...
Who will comfort me?
But the Lord remembered me and answered my prayers.
My sons have been set free.
Free from bondage.
Free from operation,
Free from chains and torture,
No longer slaves forced to work in plantations by slave masters.
My heart was filled with joy.
I waited patiently for the return of my sons.

For so many years,
not a word or sign of home coming from my sons to rebuild my land,
wipe away my tears and comfort me.
I sit in my misery and hear how great my sons have become in foreign lands.
Doctors, nurses, scientists, engineers, politicians and leaders in the great foreign lands.
Great sports men and women, musicians and actors… hmmmm.
But I have been totally forgotten, forgotten, and abandoned by my children.
Left to die in the hands of my corrupt children in my land,
who only enrich themselves and lavish my wealth
while their brothers, brethren, sisters, children, women die of hunger and starvation,
sickness and diseases. Oh, what a shame.
Now I have become like a wilderness.
The seas and deserts have once again opened their mouth,
swallowing what is left of my children in my land in their hundreds and thousands,
children, women, young men, all in the name of searching for greener pasture in foreign land.
Just to escape the hunger and starvation imposed on them by their wicked and corrupt leaders.
Not a kiss, not a hug, not a chance to say good-bye.
They have become willing slaves,
preferring to die in the seas and deserts
just to be with their siblings in foreign land,
where they will no longer know hunger and starvation, sickness and diseases.
To a land where there is no darkness,
where children are in schools not in the farms or in the streets.
Where animals and humans don’t drink water from the same pond.
Oh, what a retched and abandoned mother I have become…

Who will comfort me?
This is my agony…
I AM MOTHER AFRICA.

THE WILLING SLAVE

I grew up listening to the history of slave trade. The 'injustice' done to blacks. The 'injustice' done to Africa by the colonial masters, by the western world. Our fathers were thought the same. Now our children are still learning the same horrific history of black slavery and slave trade. These has in no little way filled most blacks with prejudice, anger, hatred, big sense of loss and negativity. We feel the entire western world owes us (blacks) everything. But I think time has come for us blacks to dispel these teachings and mind-set that has robbed us of our dignity, who we are and every sense of purpose and teach our children the whole history, the true history, the involvement and participation of black leaders. And perhaps begin to take responsibility and share blame for their part in black slavery and this inhuman slave trade.

The history of the slave trade has always begun with: the Arabs came, the British came, the Americans came, the French came, the Germans came, the Portuguese came… just to build up sentiments and lame justification for Africa's poverty, leadership incompetence and backwardness, with no mention of how Africa became a hunting ground.

It is a fact and common knowledge that before and during the period of slave trade, Africans did not have a common identity. They did not think of themselves as Africans, which sadly one can argue is still the same situation with blacks today. Ethnic, cultural and religious differences were the main reasons for waging wars and taking others – fellow blacks – as slaves. They never thought of themselves as Africans. Instead as members of their own different ethnic groups. Those being sold into slavery were regarded and considered to be 'outsiders' from the seller's own community and treating those considered to be 'outsiders' in such a way was very much acceptable.

Blacks have never been united. Before slave trade, blacks were fighting and killing each other. They were taking other tribes as prisoners of war and as slaves. The only time and place blacks did not 'fight' one another was in the plantations as slaves, because they were altogether being controlled, beaten, tortured and killed by the slave masters. Even at that, blacks still betrayed blacks. In early 1800, a black slave in Virginia, America known as Gabriel Prosser attempted a revolution, an uprising but failed because he was betrayed by two other black slaves who revealed his plan to their masters. Nelson Mandela said, "I dream of an Africa which is in peace with itself". It is then reasonable to say that I dream of blacks who are in peace with one another.

Africans usually enslaved 'other' people, not their own particular ethnic or cultural group. Slaves were taken as prisoners of war or enslaved in payment for debt or as punishment for crime. This enslavement was usually on a small scale. It was enough to supply the demand for slaves within Africa, but not enough to supply the demand from outside. As the demand from outsiders, such as Arabs and Europeans grew, warfare and raids to get slaves and the kidnapping of individuals increased. Europeans wanted to buy enslaved Africans to work on the land they owned on the Caribbean islands and in America. They chose Africans for a number of reasons, one being because they were used to farming. Also, they were physically strong but above all, because Africans were vulnerable. They had leaders who were weak, selfish, greedy, clueless, uncivilized. Leaders who were only interested in their personal wealth, power and fame. But how much has this changed, even in this 21st century? The mindset of African leaders is to accept what they are told by the western world. Africa and their leaders are still subjects to their former colonial masters.

"A true leader has the confidence to stand alone, the courage to make tough decisions, and the compassion to listen to the needs of others. He does not set out to be a leader but becomes one by the equality of his actions and the integrity of his intent" – Douglas MacArthur.

It's about time we held Africa and their leaders accountable for all the atrocities in Africa and black race if we must stamp out and conquer racial discrimination.

Most of the history of slave trade centres around the western world. African traditional chiefs, kings and slave dealers, those responsible for going into the main lands to raid houses and farms to capture slaves, those kings and chiefs who make war against other communities to capture slaves are rarely mentioned. If there was no supply, I do not think demand would have had any effect. Of course, African leaders had a choice, but their greed for personal wealth and gain blinded their eyes to this wickedness.

This book is not about what Europeans did to Africa, it is about what BLACKS have REFUSED to do for Africa. This book is not all about slave trade, its wickedness and inhuman treatment meted to Africans, meted to blacks. However, black history can never be complete without the mention of slave trade.

I do not intend to bore us with the history of slave trade, neither do I wish to reignite the sad memories, anger and hatred it brings. Not about blames. Rather, this book is about lessons, opportunities and equality slave trade has created, especially for the black race. It's about reconciliation and congregation. Not about division. Not about repatriation, but about unity and integration. To turn the negative effects of racism into positive energy to develop and build Africa, save African children. Make Africa habitable and economically independent. To help tackle African migration and its deadly consequences and ease the stress and burden it places on Europe and the western world. To create true equality between blacks and whites. However, it is the only thing that can correct one's past, build one's present and guaranty one's future. At least, that is the way I see it. The price of education is paid once, but the price of ignorance is paid for a lifetime.

Hence, determination, discipline and commitment are the key words. "Accustom yourself to look first to the dreadful consequences of failure; then fix your eye on the glorious prize which is before you; and when your strength begins to fail, and your spirits are well-nigh exhausted, let the animating view rekindle your resolution, and call forth in renewed vigour the fainting energies of your soul" —William Wilberforce.

Racism, discrimination, inequality, upper or lower class, first class or second-class citizens to a large extent, has so much to do with economy either as an individual, a nation, race or continent than the colour of your skin.

This is not about rescuing the world. This is about rescuing Africa. This is not just about fighting global inequality; this is about inequality among blacks. Blacks in the western world, blacks all over the world and blacks in Africa. Only then can blacks as a race be equals with the rest of the world.

The problem with the black race is not the colour of our skin but our mentality and loss of identity. No guts, no glory.

We blame and keep blaming imperialists. We keep blaming the western world for the woes of Africa and the black race. But to conquer external battles, internal battles must be fought and won.

We pride ourselves on our individual achievements and positions. But how much pride do we take as a people, as a race, just the way we pride ourselves in being British, French, Canadian, European or American, but never African? Martin Luther King Jr. said, "The ultimate measure of a man is not where he stands in moments of comfort and convenience, but where he stands at times of challenge and controversy."

THE POSITIVE IMPACT OF THE SLAVE TRADE

The era of slave trade was the era when humans were still in the 'process' of civilization, the process of discovering themselves and were hungry for development and creativity. Humans are only higher animals and in the animal kingdom, only the fittest survives. The geology or origin of Human or however you choose to believe humans came to be is not important to me at this stage. What is important is to understand that human development and civilization has been and still is a process. Hence, the slave trade, without any form of justification whatsoever was part of that process.

I use the words 'without justification' for those who are still emotionally and sentimentally enslaved to the memories of slave trade. The truth of the matter is that slavery was only a process and the only means for acquiring manual labour necessary at that time to carry out these developments leading to civilization. There were no technologies and machines then as we have today hence, manual labour. In doing so, some wicked-minded people made it their sole business and profited heavily by it.

Today, human trafficking is still going on, and some wicked souls are profiting from it. Drug trafficking is still going on and, on the increase. People are profiting from it; profiting from lives being destroyed. Trade in firearms, both legal and illegal, is still going on from individuals and mafia groups, including nations. We are seeing the ruins, devastations and loss of lives it leaves on its part. These forms of trade are as evil as the trade in slaves but they are still going on.

Unfortunately, African leaders were and still are sleeping when the Western world moved on and is still moving on. Some historic sympathizers would argue and tell you that America is more than 200 years old, founded on July 4th, 1776. Canada, founded on 1st July 1867.

United Kingdom, 1st May 1707. Germany, 2nd February 962 AD. Australia, 1st January 1901. London, 50 AD. Scotland, 843 AD. Italy, 17th March 1861. Netherlands, 30th January 1648.

If you make excuses for Africa not being as old as America, Great Britain, France and Germany. What then can you say about the rich and economically independent United Arab Emirates only founded on 2nd Dec 1971. The worl superpower Russia was founded on 25th December 1991, although one could argue that Russia has been of old as part of USSR. Are most African countries not older than the United Arab Emirates? Excuses are only a lazy man's apology. When purpose is not defined, abuse becomes inevitable. "Leaders think and talk about the solutions. Followers think and talk about the problems" – Brian Tracy.

The big question is, and I ask: Are the whites as a race (Western world) created, evolved, metamorphosed or came to be (whatever form of human origin you may choose or believe in) before the black race? You know the answer, the answer is NO. As a matter of fact, history tells us that human race began in Africa; particularly, central Eastern Africa. Africa is considered by most palaeontologists to be the oldest inhabited territory on Earth, with the human species originating from the continent. True or false, it's not my job to prove. It is not important to me. History also suggests that as humans began to migrate, they came across lands surrounded by waters, hostile environment and adverse weather conditions. Their survival instinct was ignited. This is where we now know as Europe. Until you are challenged in your comfort zone, your survival instinct will not be ignited. Your comfort zone can never be your throne. When a boxer gets into the ring, it's only the survival instinct that brings him out a champion. Blacks have been challenged, humiliated, degraded in every sense yet, have remained willing slaves in their 'comfort zone'. "Only you and you alone can change your situation. Don't blame it on others or anyone" – Leonardo DiCaprio.

One of the positive sides of slave trade is the seeming equality it created amongst Blacks and Whites. Equality in this context takes into account the fact that the walls of racial discrimination have been and still are being broken down. Racial discrimination is no longer what it used to be before, during and after slave trade, especially in this 21st century.

Fighting or dismantling racial discrimination has been a process, just like slave trade was a process. I do not see the sacrifice made by the victims of those horrible slave era who I call Heroes any more or less different from the sacrifice made and still being made by our fallen soldiers and those still fighting to protect you and I, and who give us sense of peace and freedom in exchange for the peace, joy and happiness of their loved ones, fathers, mothers, husbands, wives, brothers, sisters and children.

My brother, the Ras General, Stanley Onwu, wrote a song, "Lonely Soldier". Have you ever sat down to consider the feelings of a lonely soldier forgotten in the battle field? When soldiers go out to fight, they have gone to protect us as one nation and one people. Not to protect white or black, not to protect the colour of our skin but to protect us as one nation and one people. How sad and heartbreaking it is therefore for our soldiers who pay the ultimate price and sacrifice with their lives to protect us as one nation and one people while we are busy killing ourselves in the streets, all in the name of racism and racial discrimination? How sad and heartbreaking it is for the heroes of slavery, our great grandfathers who built these cities and everything we enjoy today with their blood to see that we are still shedding blood in the streets, all in the name of racism and racial discrimination?

What was Africa like, before the slave trade? What was Africa like, before colonization? African leaders have always been interested in power and wealth and not in the development of their people. African leaders worship vanity. It is this same greed for power and wealth that made the slave trade a huge success – the Western world being the beneficiaries.

Are you a slave to history or a student of history? Slaves are limited, held down, remain in bondage and never exercise self-will. Students learn, research and implement their knowledge towards achieving better goals and objectives.

To fight racial discrimination, we must first do away with racial sentiments and prejudice.

The slave trade was an activity that ultimately brought blacks and whites together.

The slave trade opened the door for blacks and whites to attend the same school, live together, inter-marry and become same citizens.

The slave trade made it possible for Blacks to be leaders in the Western world.

The slave trade gave opportunities lacking in Africa for blacks to attain greater heights in education, science and technology, sports, movies, music and entertainment, business, military. The list is endless.

Enough of negative histories. Enough of attention seeking history. Enough of history of self-pity. They did this to us, they did that to us. We have allowed a history of self-pity, attention seeking and hatred to becloud our true sense of reasoning and judgement. The history of slave trade has always begun with: the British came, the Americans came, the Arabs came, the French came, with no mention of how Africa became a hunting ground. Slavery started with African kings, and we must own up and share the blame and responsibility.

What have we as blacks done to justify – since the abolition of slave trade – that we have come of age as a race? That we are capable as a race to hold our own, stand on our feet just like America and Europe? Are we (blacks) still not depending on the Western world?

A child of American parentage, although born in Africa or any part of the world remains an American. A child born of British parents in any part of the world remains British. But a child of African parentage born in America or Britain or any part of the Western world becomes Black American or Black British with 'African parentage' hence, no longer African. What a shame. We have lost our true identity and every sense of dignity. The ability to identify and define your identity will define and determine your goal and purpose. A well-defined goal and purpose will create passion and motivation. Passion and motivation are vital ingredients for change and success.

Instead of fighting to regain our dignity by first accepting our true identity as Africans, use the knowledge we have acquired in the Western world in the areas of politics, medicine, science and technology, governance etc. to build and develop Africa just like China did. We are busy carrying cards, demonstrating and protesting to be recognized and accepted in the Western world. I don't know how realistic it is to be equals with whom you are dependent on. Such gestures only exist in dreams and imaginations. It takes grace and humility. Such a relationship is often seen as awkward. Strange bedfellows as it were.

Black discrimination is not because of black skin colour, it is as a result of black skin being associated with the poverty that is ravaging Africa. Racial respect can only be achieved through racial achievement, development and economic freedom and power. The difference between first-class and second-class citizens is that the first-class citizen is economically independent while second-class citizen is economically dependent. The first-class citizen is the leader while second-class citizen is the subject.

The harmonious co-habitation of Blacks and whites can only be achieved when Africa can offer equal opportunities to the rest of the world, just like America and Europe.

I define the slave trade era as a process towards human development and civilization. It is therefore wrong for us to keep judging the actions of the past centuries through the eyes of this century and modern civilization. William Wilberforce said, "How can we judge fairly of the characters and merits of men, of the wisdom or folly of actions, unless we have… an accurate knowledge of all particulars, so that we may live as it were in the times, and among the persons, of whom we read, see with their eyes, and reason and decide on their premises?" Past, no matter how often you visit it, there is nothing new to see.

The weak are exploited by the stronger. The truth is that the West has always been stronger mentally. Africa has always been weak mentally thereby producing mentally weak leaders, as it was in the olden days. Worse still, in this 21st century we have seen Africa producing leaders who are both mentally and physically weak. They are leaders who are either physically sick or too old to carry out the business of governance, not to mention the totally dumb and clueless corrupt ones. How then do you expect leaders who spend more time in hospitals abroad than they spend in office to lead nations of Africa to greatness and make sound decisions? Yet we all sit back and watch. How do we expect leaders who are too old and not in touch with modern technologies to lead a generation born into technology? Leaders who are not computer literate? But the good news is, through black integration in the Western world, blacks have produced and still producing mentally strong individuals and leaders. The bad news is, we have taken up positions as leaders, using our knowledge, strength and abilities only in the Western world while Africa lies in ruins.

My heart leaps with total admiration when I see young, energetic and vibrant leaders like Bill Clinton of the United States of America in his days stepping out to address the congress and the nation. Young and vibrant leaders like David Cameron of the United Kingdom. Margaret Thatcher, in her day, was vibrant and energetic. It does not matter what you think of President Vladimir Putin of Russia, his physical strength and energetic aura cannot be denied. Young leaders like Emmanuel Macron of France and Justin Pierre James Trudeau of Canada. I got chills and goose bumps when I see Former President Barrack Obama of the United States of America with his sleeves rolled up and literally jumping down the stairs of Air Force One; his aura and the audience he commands when he speaks is so amazingly electrifying. Yet, deep down in my heart, I was sad, wishing and hoping this was happening in Africa.

There is a social gap between blacks in the Western world and blacks in Africa. You are more likely to be robbed or even killed in Africa if you came from Europe, simply because they feel those in Europe are better off financially and possess good things of live. They believe blacks in Europe lead easy lives and do not lack anything. But I am yet to see or hear of anyone robbed in Europe because they're coming from Africa. Instead, you are more likely to be quarantined and screened for infections and diseases. Yet we say we're black and proud. Is that what to be proud of? I do not think so. Have you considered why African migration is ever-increasing, despite the deadly risk? It is because blacks in Africa want to be like blacks in Europe who they see as privileged and better off. Do blacks in the western world see blacks in Africa as equals? The answer is no.

Never have I seen a race so gifted, talented, strong and passionate, yet have been let down, dehumanised, demoralised and destroyed by lack of leadership and support. Black youths, both in Africa and the diaspora, have always tried to make a difference in whatever they chose to do. African youths training on sandy pitches to become great footballers yet, never appreciated, supported or recognized by their leaders but worshipped in the Western world. Athletes training without facilities and funding, yet they thrive and keep thriving to make Africa and the black race proud while their leaders are busy looting the treasury. I can't help but think of what Africa could be if sports are developed, supported in Africa like Europe? What jobs it will create for African youths? What revenue it will generate for the continent? We have more blacks representing other continents than those representing Africa. Africa keep losing her talented youths to other countries and other continents, and these countries and continents are taking all the glory.

Does Africa have any reason to be poor? Africa is poor because our mentality towards Africa as blacks is poor. Blacks are not weak people physically but we need to be strong mentally too. It is the mental weakness of African leaders that made Africa a hunting ground for slaves during the slave trade era. This same mental weakness has made blacks depend on the Western world for survival, safe-haven and comfort zone. Hence, becoming WILLING SLAVES. Unless we arise to show mental strength by identifying with Africa which is the black origin, use our wealth of knowledge to save and transform Africa, no black anywhere in the world will have respect. Unless we arise and produce leaders who are mentally and physically strong, leaders like the late King Jaja of Opobo, exploitation and discrimination of blacks will not seize. “If to be feelingly alive to the sufferings of my fellow-creatures is to be a fanatic, I am one of the most incurable fanatics ever permitted to be at large” — William Wilberforce.

RELIGION: A BANE OR BLESSING TO BLACK RACE?

Religion of any kind is supposed to point people to the right direction toward liberation; liberation from spiritual, mental, emotional and physical bondage. Religious leaders are therefore seen as the custodians of the word of God, teaching people the truth and leading by example.

I am proud of the eloquence, zeal and passion of black religious leaders (Pastors). They come out passionately to speak and condemn black segregation, killings, inequality and injustice among blacks and whites in America, Britain, Europe and all over the Western world. They lead protests for one black killed in the Western world but stand back and watch while blacks die in their hundreds and thousands from police brutality and killings, hunger and starvation, sickness and diseases, religious and ethnic killings, wicked leadership and corruption that is ravaging Africa. African migrants are dying in their hundreds and thousands trying to cross the Mediterranean and Sahara Desert yet, I haven't seen them speak or mobilize their members, lead protests against African leaders, the black origin. Neither have we lead protests, match to the airports and hospitals in Europe demanding that African leaders who have refused to build hospitals in Africa, but come to Europe for treatment while poor black children die of preventable sicknesses and diseases due to lack of Medicare, be sent back to Africa. No, it's not our cup of tea because we do not live in Africa.

The story of Moses in the Bible is being taught in every congregation and every church. So many books have been written on the life of Moses and the children of Israel. I believe the story of Moses was written for the black race. Moses, in modern times could be regarded as an 'unaccompanied child migrant' who was born of slave parents, just like most blacks.

I do not intend to bore anyone with the story of Moses,

but I do not take for granted that everyone is familiar with it, especially the lessons and its relevance to Black history and black race.

Moses was born into trouble, in the land of slavery. It was a nation under the leadership of a wicked leader, a murderer; a leader who had no respect for the lives of children and the rule of law. A land where his parents were slaves. He was smuggled out of his house as a baby by his parents, placed in a colt and pushed into the river (just like the migration crises we have today). Exodus chapter 2: 1-3. Because the king of Egypt made law demanding all male children born of slave parents be killed, to stop slaves from increasing and becoming too powerful.

Moses was found and rescued by Pharaoh's daughter and her maids and was taken to Pharaoh's palace. Although he had all the privileges of a prince and a king to be, because Pharaoh's daughter adopted him as her son, the Bible records that Moses refused to be called the son of Pharaoh's daughter.

> *"By faith Moses, when he was come to years,*
> *refused to be called the son of Pharaoh's daughter"*
> *Hebrews 11:24 (kjv).*

He refused to lose his identity because he was constantly being told by his sister and mother where he came from. He refused to be called an Egyptian or 'Hebrew-Egyptian'. This is the first problem of the black race. We have lost our identity, preferring to be called Black American, Black British, Black this, Black that. Anything other than African. What a shame. How would religious leaders who don't know who they are or accept and identify with who they are teach others the truth? How do you expect parents to teach their children the truth when they themselves do not know who they are?

The problem of the black race is the respect and equality that we seek can never be found or achieved in the Western world but in Africa through quality leadership and development. Personal achievement(s), no matter how big or small can never guarantee racial equality and respect.

Moses was not driven by personal ambition and achievement of becoming the king of the most powerful nation on the planet. He did not establish a church, preaching and promising the children of Israel who were in bondage prosperity in Egypt, taking tithes and offerings and enriching himself, buying private jets and mansions like most black pastors do today. He had golden opportunities of becoming the next Pharaoh, yet he knew that racial equality lies in empowering his people economically. Not in Egypt but in Canaan. The Bible says, *"My people perish for lack of knowledge…" Hosea 4:6*

Until Blacks know who they are, solve their identity crises, identify with Africa and exchange personal achievements for racial economic achievements, developments and empowerment, Blacks all over the world will remain second-class citizens, regardless of personal heights and individual achievements, position or status.

How did we Blacks become part of the Western community? Just the same way the children of Israel became part of the Egyptian community: SLAVERY.

Joseph, in Genesis Chapter 37, was sold into slavery by his brothers, the same way our forefathers were sold into slavery by their leaders and brothers. Joseph had special talents and soon found himself in the corridors of power in Egypt. He saw an opportunity to become the prime minister of the most powerful nation in the world. Rising from prison to palace and from a slave boy to prime minister was, to him, the greatest achievement.

But, unlike Moses, he placed personal ambition and achievement and the welfare of his immediate family over national and racial economic achievement, freedom and development of his people who were suffering from hunger and starvation. He used his privilege just for himself and his immediate family by bringing them over to

Egypt – a 'dream land'. A more developed nation. A rich nation. Little did he know it was a bad idea. He never thought of using his skills, talent, knowledge of leadership acquired in Egypt to build the economy of his nation, Canaan, (Genesis Chapter 42). He forgot and abandoned where he came from – his people, his race – instead, acquired the citizenship of Egypt. Typical of blacks.

The big question is: did his personal achievement as prime minister in Egypt guarantee equality between his people, the Canaanites and the Egyptians? The answer is NO. Are blacks doing anything different from what Joseph did? The answer is NO. Did the presidency, eloquence and achievements of President Barack Obama as the first black president of the United States of America bring respect, equality and end racial discrimination against blacks in America? The answer is NO. Racial equality does not come by personal political and economic achievement but by racial, economic and political achievement and development.

Moses understood that only good leadership and economic achievement for his race could guarantee equality and respect, not his personal ambition and achievement as king of Egypt. Sadly, Blacks in the Western world are still concerned with personal achievement rather than racial achievement. Little wonder we're still fighting for and demanding respect, equality and recognition rather than commanding respect.

Most Black pastors, both in the Western world and Africa, are more concerned with personal wealth, driving bulletproof cars and flying on private jets while African children cannot go to school and have no food to eat. They do not even have clean water to drink or a place to lay their heads. In Africa, people pay more tithes and offerings to churches and pastors than they pay taxes to the government. Even when they do pay taxes, it ends up in government officials' pockets and personal accounts. The tithes and offerings they give to churches only end up with pastors acquiring private jets and mansions all over the world. Build schools that the poor members of the congregation who are giving all that they have cannot afford.

I once went to a mechanic garage for my car servicing. There I met three other men, neatly dressed, having a discussion while their Mercedes Benz was being attended to by the auto mechanic. My attention was drawn to them, not because of their car or clothes but by the issue they were discussing, although their dressing confirmed the issue of discuss. They were pastors from one of the 'biggest' Pentecostal churches in Africa. I could feel the pain, anger and disappointment in their tone even as they tried to speak in low voices.

"I am leaving," one said. "I can't take it any longer." He paused.

"I gave everything. I gave my best, for the past fifteen years. I was with this ministry (church) from start till now. Yet my son was denied admission into the church's university simply because I could not afford the fees."

"But you are a pastor in that church?" said another man.

"Yes, I am" he said with a heavy sigh, shaking his head from left to right.

This is a church I know too well and know that the senior pastor of that church who they refer to as 'president' flies in private jets, yet his pastors cannot afford to have their children attend the university built by members. I could relate to their feelings of despair, pain and anger because it's just one story too many, haven been in a similar situation myself.

We have been in the generation of Joseph (willing slave mentality) now is the time to move on to the Moses generation (racial liberation mentality and leadership mentality). We need youths and a generation that will see themselves as Africans, not just blacks irrespective of where you were born and the colour of your passport. So long as you are black you are an African. A generation of leaders who will use their knowledge acquired in the

Western world to develop and build Africa. Only a true African dream can checkmate African-European dream (African migration).

I believe if there is anything possible anywhere in the Western world, in terms of development and achievement, it is possible in Africa. Europe and America were built on ideologies and values, commitment and dedication to race. Abraham Lincoln said, "My dream is of a place and a time when America will once again be seen as the last best hope of earth."

African leaders have failed Africa and the black race. Only 'Westernised' blacks can help to checkmate Western influence on Africa and bring the rule of law, true democracy, values and wealth creation to Africa. If we, as blacks in the Western world, cannot rise and lead Africa and stop the exploitation of Africa by the Western world, then we are part of the problem. We are part of the exploiters because we live in the Western world and are benefiting directly or indirectly from these exploitations, and are equally as guilty as the frontline exploiters.

We have been fighting for the evil which holds one race superior and another inferior to be dismantled. But I say that the superiority or inferiority of any nation or race is not determined by the colour of their skin but by the economy of that nation or race.

Not long ago, the name China was synonymous with poverty. Introducing a one child policy was the height of desperation towards building their economy. They went from making fake and substandard goods to becoming a world leader in manufacturing today with their gross domestic product standing at 11.2 trillion USD in 2016. Every nation of the world today wants trade deals with China. Her citizens no longer have the stigma of 'Economic Migrants', rather they have been glorified to the statutes of tourists, students, highly skilled workers, partners in science and technology, research and other projects. They are welcomed and respected abroad.

LIONS EATING LIONS

We preach diversity and equality but what I see is the preaching of diversity and equality for only the privileged. Yes, only for the privileged blacks who are fortunate enough to be born in or migrated to the Western world. Equality can only be true when there is no difference between blacks in Africa and blacks in the Western world. Equality can only make sense when black children in Africa have access to good education, quality healthcare, clean and available drinking water, good food and shelter and electricity just like black children in the Western world.

Equality can only make sense when Africa becomes a consumer of labour and no longer a major exporter of labour. Equality and diversity can only make sense when Africa becomes a host continent where citizens of the Western world and race can come to live, work and make a living with the assurance of good education for their children and quality healthcare.

Equality can only exist when citizens of other races are comfortable enough to acquire African citizenship with the right to vote and be voted for in Africa, not just the few missionaries, charity workers and expatriates in Africa. Until blacks in Africa can travel freely just like blacks in Western world without the stigma of economic migrants, our shout for equality and diversity will only be for our selfish interests and only for the privileged Blacks and not for the totality of the black race.

My idea of equality as a black man is not to walk freely without molestation, without discrimination as a citizen of the Western world. My idea of equality as a black man is to see Africa as a continent, the continent of the black race, black heritage becomes equal to the Western world and other developed nations of the world; not "I" as an individual, but "WE" as a race and as a continent. Abraham Lincoln said, "Don't worry when you are not recognized but strive to be worthy of recognition."

We as blacks have used the slave trade and slavery both as weapon and tool for blackmail, blackmailing other races and teaching black children the same, instead of using it as a tool for motivation in the development of Africa.

The history of the slave trade is so sensitive and has been described with so many adjectives like 'wicked', 'evil', 'barbaric', 'inhuman'… it is a phenomenon that is so thick that you can literally touch the anger and passion it evokes.

But here is my problem, how much anger and passion has it evoked in the hearts of blacks to identify with Africa?

How much anger and passion has it evoked in the hearts of blacks to rebuild Africa?

How much anger and passion has it evoked in the hearts of blacks to make and develop Africa like Europe?

How much anger and passion has it evoked in the hearts of blacks to challenge us to rise to the suffering of African children?

How much anger and passion has it evoked in the hearts of blacks to fight against corrupt and unqualified African leaders and take over the governance of Africa?

But I say this: It is no longer what Europe did to Africa; it is what blacks have refused to do for Africa.

I like the phrase 'Black lives matter'. But it's like a well-orchestrated music with a good melody but performed to the wrong audience.

Black lives should matter first to blacks.

Black lives should matter first to black leaders.

Black lives should matter first to blacks who have lost, forsaken and abandoned their true identity and heritage as Africans.

Black lives should matter first to blacks who are leaders in the Western world but cannot dream of leading Africa.

Black lives should matter first to blacks who have embraced the unholy culture of gangsterism, killing one another.

Black lives should matter first to blacks in Africa killing fellow blacks. South Africans killing fellow blacks. The horrific genocides of Rwanda and Nigeria (Northern Hausas vs Eastern Igbos). Muslims against Christians. Tribal and ethnic killings all over African countries. Lions eating Lions.

Black lives should matter first to African leaders who steal billions while watching African children die of hunger and starvation and from preventable sicknesses and diseases.

Black lives should matter first to blacks (human traffickers) who wickedly take money from poor Africans – women, children, men, young and old – put them on an inflated tube and push them off into the high seas towards Europe, a journey which thousands never made.

We display in museums weapons, chains, guns, whips used by White slave masters, but we rarely display bows and arrows used by African kings and chiefs and their warriors to fight, kill and capture fellow blacks from their farms and homes, taking them as slaves and sold.

We get angry and emotional when we see objects like bronze pots used as means of payment and exchange for slaves. And we ask how much wickedness and heartlessness, callousness it was to purchase a whole human being with these worthless objects?

I think the question should be: what is the life of a black worth to African leaders? What is the value of a human life worth to blacks who were responsible for capturing, killing and selling fellow blacks for mare objects like mirror, glass, bronze wares, pieces of cloth, guns, gun powder and brandy?

Even now, what is the life of a black worth to African leaders who sit back and watch thousands of blacks – men, women, children and youths – perish in the Mediterranean Sea and Sahara Desert trying to flee hunger and starvation in Africa?

What is the life of a black worth to us blacks in the western world, being leaders in the western world while

Africa is decaying? Let's stop transferring our aggression, frustration and anger to other races and channel our energy towards making Africa great by becoming great leaders of Africa in Africa, the continent of the black race.

If we cannot sing this song, play it loud, drum and shout it loud to African leaders, black leaders and blacks all over the world then we have no moral justification to even whisper it to the ears of the Western world.

We need a black race where all blacks will see themselves as one: 'Africans'. Not a race divided by culture, tradition, religion and ethnic sentiments. How can anyone explain that people of the same colour are divided by nationality, instead of being united by race?

I have no issues with 'Black History Month' celebrations, which have become a norm and fashion especially for blacks in diaspora. But the truth is that it is nothing other than a renewal of our mental weakness as a race and a constant reminder of 'black identity' as descendants of slaves.

Why must we keep humiliating black children – even those yet un-born – portraying them as descendants of slaves even in the eyes of their pairs in the Western world? Are we now questioning why black children who knew nothing about the slave trade are being humiliated and discriminated against? Blacks were not the only ones who went through slavery. Britain did. America did. So did India. But we would accuse other races of racism if they set out a day for themselves and their race?

Respect as a race will always elude us (blacks) if we refuse now to put the history of the slave trade and black race in proper perspective and teach our youths and children and encourage and empower them to embrace their true identity and heritage as Africans. If we refuse to teach and build them to become great leaders and save Africa from sickness and diseases, hunger and starvation, illiteracy, religious and ethnic killings, corruption, greed and wickedness and bad leadership. Africa will soon become history and black race will become 'stateless race'.

The way to rise is to fall. Africa fell through our forefathers, but we have refused to rise. If we can forgive our forefathers for their wicked involvement in the slave trade, then we must forgive all who participated in that wicked and inhuman act, including the Western world. It is important to understand that that was the level of civilization then. The world has moved on, we must move on too. Unfortunately, the black race has refused to move on and build Africa like Europe. Instead it has chosen to switch identity, depend on Western world and remain willing slaves and second-class citizens.

Black slaves

During the slave trade era, slaves were captured, sold, bought, forced onto ships in chains and fetters and taken abroad. Now, our fellow blacks willingly pay human traffickers who pack them into inflatable tubes and onto the high seas without chains and shackles under inhuman conditions, to serve as slaves in Europe while we sit and watch them perish in the seas. To date, Africa has been a major exporter of humans. Does that make anyone proud to be black? I do not think so. If we blamed the Western world for forcefully taking Africans as slaves, who do we now blame for Africans willingly begging to be slaves in Europe?

African Migrants

The history of the slave trade must always be told but no longer of hatred and discrimination and prejudice. It should be put right and correct the greed for wealth and power, wickedness and the weakness of African leaders. A history that can challenge our physical, mental, spiritual and emotional strength towards positive creativity and greatness. A history that will challenge blacks to rise and command respect rather than demand respect.

Going forward, we must allow the events of the past remain with history. Blacks must not remain slaves to history and rather should be a force to be reckoned with by history. Until we shift our focus from personal and individual achievement and glory to a focus on racial achievement, empowerment and glory, we can never be free from racial discrimination. The harmonious co-habitation of blacks and whites can only be achieved when Africa can offer equal opportunities to the rest of the world, just like America and Europe.

THE GREAT SACRIFICE

Thomas Clarkson (1760 – 1846)

William Wilberforce (1759 – 1833)

We are quick to remember, shout and broadcast all the negative things done to blacks in the Western world but we never remember, appreciate, broadcast or celebrate all the good things, opportunities and sacrifices made by other races towards blacks and the black race.

We gather to remember a black man killed, our grandparents killed during slavery, what they went through to make us who we are today in the Western world. But we never remember people of other races, those who fought for our grandparents' freedom, even with their lives, that paved the way for us to become who we are today in the Western world. We don't carve their names on stones and marbles. We don't write their names on plaque. We don't even mention their names, neither do we visit or lay wreath on their graves. Nor do we raise statues in their memory in our communities. We never mention them as being part of black history.

According to *The Mirror* published on 13 February 2018, a tweet by the Treasury stated that the sum of £20 million was borrowed from the Treasury by the British government in 1833 – 40% of its national budget, equivalent of £2,264 million today – to compensate slave dealers as part of the deal to set slaves free. This was to give slaves – black slaves, African slaves – their freedom, which was paid off only recently in 2015 by tax payers.

There have been mixed feelings about this, whether it was morally right to compensate these slave dealers rather than the slaves? Whether it was morally right to make the descendants of these slaves living in Britain contribute to this payment through taxes, rather than being compensated? Whatever side of the argument you are on, the fact that my freedom was paid for by the tax payers leaves me with nothing but the utmost gratitude and appreciation. Hence, any contribution I have made is one that I am more than happy to make.

I can understand when it comes to the issue of slave trade and slavery that we allow emotional sentiments to becloud our every sense of reasoning. For those who would crucify me, before you do, my question is: how much did African tribal chiefs and kings who were responsible for and the major beneficiaries of this evil act pay for our freedom? How much did African leaders pay for our freedom? How much did African countries pay to buy our freedom?

I am not celebrating the trauma of slavery and British involvement in the slave trade. No, I am celebrating that my freedom was paid for in Britain by the British government and the British tax payers which no African nation or government did or will ever do.

I am not celebrating the first black American president of the United States of America. I am celebrating Americans for giving a black man the opportunity to be their president.

I am not celebrating our individual achievements in the Western world, I am celebrating the opportunity the Western world has given to us to achieve these things and be what we want.

I am not proud of racial discrimination, neither am I celebrating injustices against blacks but I am celebrating my freedom of speech which gives me the right and opportunity to speak against these vices, freedom of speech and justice which are alien to African leaders.

I am not celebrating blacks being gunned down and stabbed to death in the streets of the Western world, especially in America and Britain, but I am celebrating the opportunity given to black children to have free and quality education, to be and become whatever they want to and can be. The opportunity that has produced a black president in the most influential nation of the world. The opportunity that has produced so many blacks in Western politics and governance, movies, sports and entertainment.

I am celebrating people of other races that have been strengthening the hands of blacks, lending their voices, their resources and their lives for equality, freedom and justice for all irrespective of colour, gender or religion. Celebrating the likes of Sir William Wilberforce; Lord

Grenville; Thomas Clarkson; George Fox; Martin Luther King; George Washington; Frederick Douglas of United States of America; white women activists like Hannah More; Mary Wollstonecraft; Mary Birkett and more. Africans like Ignatius Sancho; African slaves like Olaudah Equiano, a slave boy from where is now known as Nigeria; Ottabah Cugoano, a slave from where we know today as Ghana. All of whom made it possible for blacks to walk freely without molestations. Whatever citizenship and position we hold in the Western world has been given and not earned.

On 23 February 1807, Sir William Wilberforce's successful abolition bill was passed and on 25 March of the same year, the Slave Trade Act received the Royal assent. This abolished the slave trade but did not set slaves free. It wasn't until 26 July 1833 that an act was passed and came into force to set slaves free in Britain. Sir William Wilberforce died three days after – on 29 July 1833 – due to failing health. Hence, compensations and payments were made to slave dealers by the British government to buy our freedom. Fighting for you and me. I could feel the joy in William Wilberforce's heart as he lay in his sick bed. His terminal illness never stopped him from fighting for black freedom, the abolition of slave trade and the slavery of blacks. I could hear him saying; "Now my soul can finally rest in peace. My work is done. My eyes have seen this day that blacks have been set free," even as he breathed his last. How much of these people's lives, contributions and sacrifice do blacks and black children know?

Thomas Clarkson, together with eleven other abolitionists formed The Society for Effecting the Abolition of Slave Trade in May 1787. He dedicated his life to the abolition and freedom of black slaves, not only in Britain but also throughout Europe and America. He risked his life gathering evidence, witnesses and drumming up support across Europe. Of course, he was hated by slave dealers. Several assassination attempts were made on his life. He was attacked and escaped being thrown overboard slave ships. In 1837, his only child was killed in an accident aged forty. Yet Clarkson continued fighting for the freedom of black slaves. In June 1840, a convention was held in London, championed by the 'British and Foreign Anti-Slavery Society' to abolish slave trade throughout the world and Thomas Clarkson was voted president of that convention, wherein 5,000 delegates and observers from Britain were in attendance. Other countries in attendance were the United States of America, Spain, Canada, West Indies, Switzerland and France. They all came together to abolish slavery worldwide. Thomas Clarkson died on the 26th of September 1846 at the age of eighty-six. How much of this selfless man do blacks know and celebrate?

Olympe de Gouges was a white female activist and writer who fought for equal rights for women and men including blacks. In 1788 she released a pamphlet 'Reflections on Black People, where she wrote as follows:

"Why are black people enslaved?

The colour of people's skin only suggests a slight difference.

There is no discord between day and night,

the sun and the moon and between the stars and dark sky.

All is varied; it is the beauty of nature. Why destroy nature's work?"

Olympe de Gouges got married at the tender age of sixteen but did not know the joy of matrimony as her husband died shortly after. She vowed not to remarry but devoted her time and life fighting for justice, fighting against slavery, fighting for the black race and black freedom. She was white and not black. Yet, we do not remember, appreciate or mention her and her likes in black history. How much of her and her sacrifice do blacks know and appreciate?

Abraham Lincoln 16th U.S. President (1809 -1865)

How much of the likes of President Abraham Lincoln do blacks know, appreciate and celebrate, who in 1863, issued the Emancipation Proclamation declaring all slaves free. Of course, we know that the slave trade still did not end but he was relentless in his fight for the freedom of slaves. He recognized that the Emancipation Proclamation must be enshrined into the Constitution in order to have legal powers. Hence, the 13th amendment to the United States of America Constitution of 1865 which states, "Neither slavery nor involuntary servitude, except as a punishment for crime whereof the party shall have been duly convicted, shall exist within the United States, or any place within their jurisdiction."

America may not have bought our freedom or paid compensation to American slave dealers and owners like Britain did, but for four years (1861-1865), under the leadership of President Abraham Lincoln, America fought a civil war for the emancipation and freedom of all slaves (blacks). There were more than half a million casualties and about 360,000 deaths were recorded on the side of the federal government fighting for slave freedom and equality. There were about 483,000 casualties and about 258,000 deaths recorded on the side of Confederate.

Yet, I do not remember all those killed in that civil war being only blacks. These were white Americans, giving their lives to make us (blacks) equals and free. Not counting the huge financial cost of more than $15 billion. Neither was I told, read and still cannot remember any black being among the 119 Congress members that defeated the remaining 56 in a 119-56 vote in favour of the abolition of the Slave Trade Act and freedom for all slaves on January 31, 1865. If am right, they were all white Americans. How much of these people do we know? How much of these people do we remember? How much of these people do we appreciate? How much of these people do we celebrate?

Less than a week after the war was officially declared over and the Southern Confederate general Robert E Lee surrendered on 9 April 1865, President Abraham Lincoln was assassinated. He was shot while attending a performance at Ford's Theatre in Washington DC by a member of the Confederacy – those opposed to the abolition of slavery. He died the next morning on 15 April 1865. He and over half a million Americans died for our freedom; for the freedom of black race. How much of these sacrifices do we remember, appreciate and celebrate?

Not every American was involved in the slave trade. Not every Briton was involved in the slave trade. Not every European was involved in the slave trade. Yet we do not find the need to celebrate those, despite not being black, who fought for our freedom; the black race's freedom. Black history is like a horror movie with a happy ending. The actors are not the slave masters. The real actors and my heroes are those who made the sacrifice, even risking their lives to bring an end to this horrific sad tale. We focus on the pain of past slavery that we don't appreciate and celebrate the freedom of today and the huge sacrifice made by other races.

If there is a period to be remembered by blacks, if there is a period to be celebrated by blacks and by the whole world, it should be the period that slave trade was abolished worldwide, and blacks given their freedom – June 1840. The year of peace. The year of unity and equality. The year that blacks and whites became same citizens.

Celebrating this period with joy, with carnivals with banners, appreciating other races for their contributions and sacrifice towards the abolition of slave trade and slavery and opportunities given to blacks to become citizens of the world. Perhaps, this might take away the bitter hatred that the negative teaching of the slave trade has created over the years in the hearts of blacks. Perhaps, this might remove the deadly rivalry amongst Whites and Blacks and create unity and harmony, friendliness amongst Blacks and Whites, especially among youths and children. "If friendship is your weakest point then you are the strongest person in the world" – Abraham Lincoln.

This is what we should be celebrating, no longer the history of hatred and self-pity that has always divided us.

THE LOST GENERATION

We are black and proud but not proud to be Africans. Some are not even proud to be black. What makes you an indigene is your gene (genetic factor). Where you were born can make you a citizen, but your gene is what makes you an indigene. If your gene is black, then you are African.

There is no black heritage other than Africa. We have disowned and abandoned our heritage, exchanging our heritage for silver and gold and have remained 'willing slaves'. The fact that you are African American means you are first African before being American. That you are Black British means you are first African before being British, or whatever nationality you hold.

We sit and mourn and demonstrate over non-inclusion of blacks at the Oscars, at the Grammys, at the MOBOs and all the awards. What a shame. Who are the ones making Hollywood great? Who are the ones making music and entertainment great in America and Europe? Who are the people who make sports great in America and Europe?

I was watching a basketball tournament with my kids some time ago. It was America's basketball team playing against Nigeria's basketball team. And my six-year-old daughter asked me:

"Dad, what team is Nigeria and what team is America?"

I told her, "The ones in green jerseys are the Nigerian team and the ones in white jerseys are the American team."

She went on.

"But they are all blacks, what's the difference and why are they playing against themselves?"

I paused for a while, took a deep breath.

It was difficult explaining to my six-year-old daughter that people of the same colour, same heritage and the same race, are disunited, divided and disorientated, mentally, emotionally and physically by nationalities.

I had to explain to her that the ones in green jerseys are Black Africans (Nigerian team) while the ones in white jerseys are Black Americans (American team) or African American as they prefer to be called. It took me days trying to explain to her young mind how this has come to be, hence the history of the slave trade.

Reaching for her American passport and Nigerian passport, I went on to explain to her:

"You are an American by nationality because you were born in America and Nigerian (African) by heritage because I am Nigerian by origin and heritage. This means you have dual citizenship; you can function as an African or American, depending on your values."

You wouldn't think it was that easy to make her young mind understand, would you? How many millions of black children like my daughter are confused, don't know who they are and where they belong?

I once went to my son's college in Manchester in the United Kingdom. I met some of his friends, black kids. As we were all having a chat, I asked some of them where they came from. They looked bewildered. I realized it was a difficult question for them. I was glad when one of them answered.

"I am British."

Then my next question, "Your parents, where are they from?"

If I thought the first question was confusing, I was wrong because this time there was lots of eye contact with one another, kicking and poking each other to answer. All I could get from this lovely fifteen-year old boy was:

"My parents are from Africa."

Some were more direct in naming the country in Africa where their parents come from but had no idea or clue where that was. I felt so sorry and sad for the continent of Africa, the black race and the 'lost generations'.

How long shall we continue to allow black children to go through the humiliation of identity crises? Not knowing who they are or where they belong? The places they call 'home' rejects them and treat them as outcasts and slaves yet, we still reject black origin-African heritage?

This is the missing link. Parents, in their bid to give their children a 'great future', have erased African heritage and identity from the history of the slave trade, preferring to be called blacks but not Africans. We have successfully replaced the word 'Africans' with just 'Blacks'. Africans for blacks in Africa and Blacks for blacks in the Western world. Some, despite being told by their parents, decided to erase African heritage from their history and their generations.

But one thing is clear, America, Britain and other Western countries that we see as better, richer and more civilized than Africa – the western countries we now claim as our own – were built by someone, some people, ideologies, belief, passion and vision.

Sometimes I ask myself, why the Western slave masters, having discovered fertile land, black slaves who were strong and used to farming, a continent rich in mineral resources, gold, oil, great climatic condition and warm weather, great wildlife and rich tropical rain forests you just name it, did not see the need to settle in Africa and instead, took all they could to build and develop their continents and race?

The answer is passion; passion and vision for their heritage. How much passion do we as blacks have for our heritage? What is our vision for the black race and black heritage? It was passion and vision for heritage that saw Moses in the Bible refusing to be called an Egyptian, refusing to become Pharaoh in Egypt, instead using his knowledge acquired in Egypt and the leadership skills acquired in the Pharaoh's palace to lead his people out of bondage and rebuild their shattered heritage.

Sometimes I ask myself what the fate of the black race would have been if not for our fathers and forefathers who gave their lives fighting for the independence of the various countries of Africa: Dr. Nnamdi Azikiwe; Chief Obafemi Awolowo and Sir Ahmadu Bello of Nigeria, supported by Chief Mrs. Funmilayo Ransom Kuti.

Ghana's big Six: Dr. Kwame Nkrumah who became the prime minister and first president of Ghana; Joseph Boakye Danquah-founding member of the United Gold Coast Convention (UGCC) founded on August 4, 1947. Dr. Edward Akufo-Addo-founding member of the UGCC, who later became Chief justice and president of Ghana. Also, Emmanuel Obetsebi-Lamptey-founding member of the UGCC. Ebenezer Ako-Adjei-founding member of the UGCC. Dr. Nelson Mandela of South Africa; Jomo Kenyatta-the first prime minister and the first president of Kenya; Leopold Senghor of Senegal, King Jaja of Opobo, just to name a few.

What if these people all decided to throw away their African heritage and identity and exchange it for Western citizenship and heritage? They had every opportunity and excuse to do this, yet they laid down their lives for the freedom of Africa. Not only did they fight for the independence of Africa, they became leaders in Africa. Today, instead of fighting to liberate Africa from wicked leaders, save Africa from hunger and starvation, rebuild African heritage by becoming leaders in Africa, we are fighting to be recognized, accepted and become leaders in the Western world. Only your gene can make you an indigene.

We can give one million and one excuses why we cannot associate with or build Africa. Why we are blacks and not Africans? Because we were born in the Western world and the Western world is our home. Yes, Moses in the Bible had excuses too. He told God he was a stammerer, (not eloquent in speech). He was not burn in Hebrew land, neither did he grow up in Hebrew land. He was born in Egypt and knew next to nothing about his land of origin and nativity, about his heritage or where his parents came from. Just like most blacks in the Western world.

Physically speaking, what was one rode in Moses hand compared to the 'great' magicians of the Pharaoh and their army? Moses knew this. His fellow countrymen he was trying to help settle issues ridiculed him and called him a murderer, asking him who made him a judge and a ruler over them…

"And when he went out the second day,

behold, two men of the Hebrews strove together:

and he said to him that did the wrong, wherefore smitest thou thy fellow?

And he said, Who made thee a prince and a judge over us?

Intendest thou to kill me as you killed the Egyptian?

And Moses feared, and said, surely this thing is known"

(Exodus chapter 2: 14 and 15)

His own people rebelled against him, made for themselves images and elected leaders for themselves while he was up on the mounting for their sake, yet that did not stop him. A famous blind person was once asked what could be worse than blindness; he said, "Having eyes without having a vision." A man with a vision is like a mad man, no one understands him. Nothing can stop vision, only lack of it. Death cannot stop vision and passion. Oppositions cannot stop a man with a vision.

The Bible says, "Write down the vision and make it plain on tablets so that a runner can carry the correct message to others"– Habakkuk 2:2 (New Living Translation).

By writing this, I know and believe, even while I am gone that someday, someone will read it, carry the correct message and run with it to save Africa and the Black Race. Build Africa just like America and Europe and restore the black heritage and dignity. This is the reason why I love the book, The *Audacity of Hope* by former U.S. president and the first black president of the United States of America… Barack Obama. Oh, how I wished (blacks) would have that same audacity to accept their identity and heritage as Africans and fight with every blood in their vein to deliver Africa from bad leadership and from corruption.

That you are a movie star cannot stop you from becoming a leader, ask Ronald Regan and Arnold Schwarzenegger. That you are an entertainer cannot stop you from becoming a world-class leader, ask Donald Trump. You don't need to be a politician to be a leader and fight for Africa.

Sometimes I wonder what Africa would be if all the black governors and senators in America (African Americans) were governors and senators and presidents in Africa?

If all the black members of parliament (MPs) and local council chairmen and mayors in the United Kingdom (Black British) were MPs and local council chairmen, prime ministers and presidents in Africa? If all the black Western human rights activists were activists in Africa, fighting for the rights of helpless African children, women and youths? If former president Barack Obama was president in Africa, think of what Africa would be? If some of the big and influential black pastors in America and Europe were presidents, governors and senators in Africa, think of what Africa would be? Think of what

Africa would be if all the youths and young graduates from the best universities in America and Europe became leaders in Africa instead of carrying cards and protesting in the streets of America and Europe for 'equal rights and justice?' Think of what Africa would be if all the black musicians and entertainers in America, the United Kingdom and Europe had their studios in Africa? If the African American Hollywood stars, actors and actresses were doing what they do best in Africa and organizing their own awards rather than protesting for non-inclusion in the Western awards? Talk about job creation, employment and development. I might be a dreamer, but so was Martin Luther King Jr. when he said, "I have a dream…"

When will blacks know and understand that protests alone cannot guarantee equality? When will blacks learn and understand that protest is a sign of weakness and inferiority? It's good to protest, it is good to fight racial inequality but, it is far better to challenge and take back control from corrupt African leaders who have made blacks willing slaves and economic migrants. Rebuild Africa and make Africa and the black race great again.

We are quick to protest because we live in a modern

and civilized society (the Western world), where there's the rule of law, human rights and freedom of speech. While our fellow blacks, men, women and children living in Africa do not have the luxury of freedom of speech and human rights. Who will give them a voice? Who'll make Africa a 'sane' society? Who'll deliver Africa from the hands of visionless, corrupt and wicked leaders?

There is a continent that is in dying and dire need of leadership; a continent in dire need of true governance; a continent whose resources are wasting and being wasted by unqualified and corrupt leaders. There is a continent whose youths are in dire need of direction and help. There is a continent whose children are not being treated better than animals and need saving. There is a continent with great potential to be as rich as the Western world yet, is one of the poorest in the whole world. There is a continent in dire need of your knowledge and leadership. I dare say, if blacks think they have anything to offer in governance and leadership in the Western world, there is a continent that needs it. That is the continent of Africa, the continent of the black race.

Moses in the Bible did not choose protest(s) as his strategy, he chose leadership; leadership of his race not of Egypt.

I watched with heavy heart, anger and disappointment during the 50th anniversary of the death of Martin Luther King Jr. as blacks in America came together, referring to themselves and being referred to as 'The new generation of protesters.' What a shame.

The Windrush scandal of 2018 in Britain was not only a shame to African leaders but a shame to all blacks. It is totally unacceptable to treat any human being with disrespect, cruelty and discrimination. The Windrush scandal was one of many instances where blacks have been humiliated, mentally, emotionally and physically tortured. Blacks were detained, reduced to nothing and wasted in a place they thought they belonged; in a place they thought would protect them; in a place where they were promised safety, a new life and a home.

In the midst of all these, I could not contain my uneasiness and feelings of frustration and anger as I watched African leaders (the Jamaican Prime Minister and Caribbean leaders) and black members of parliament in United Kingdom trying to show their anger and disappointment at the British government. They were talking with passion against the treatment mated to the Windrush generation and demanding compensation.

Then I asked myself, if Jamaica was like Britain, would Jamaicans not be proud and happy to live and work in Jamaica? If Jamaica was like Britain would there have been this Windrush embarrassment, scandal and humiliation? Yet their leaders were not ashamed to show their faces, neither did they have the decency to accept responsibility for the humiliation and embarrassment meted to black families through their poor and irresponsible leadership.

Again, watching some black British Members of Parliament talk with anger and passion, I could not help but wonder and imagine if they were leaders in Africa, developing and creating jobs then Jamaica and indeed Africa, would be just like Britain or even better. Yes, the British government failed these families, humiliated and betrayed them but the Caribbean and African leaders have not only failed the black race but have exposed the black race to these modern-day slavery, humiliation and torture. We all (blacks) should bury our heads in shame.

I dream of a generation of blacks who'll focus on building the black race (Africa). A generation of leaders who will lead the government of Africa. Not a generation of protesters but a generation of producers. A generation who will not see themselves just as blacks but a generation who will see themselves as Africans.

Just like King Jaja of Opobo, Dr. Nelson Mandela and more, it is more honourable to die as a leader in Africa, developing Africa and giving Africa economic freedom which will take away black discrimination and racial humiliation all over the world, than die in the streets of Western world as a victim of hate crime or as a protester. Which sadly, has claimed and still claiming lives of thousands of black youths. Most black youths who engage in crime or drug use in the Western world do so because they are frustrated. They don't know who they are or where they belong. The place they call home does not treat them as one.

We have been through the stages of the slave trade, yet we are not free from slavery. We have been through the stages of colonization, yet we are still dependent on the colonial masters. We have been through post-independence wars yet we still do not know peace. We are now in the era of political mismanagement. I am not interested in the history of the slave trade and its destructive effects on Africa. I am interested in its positive effects on the black race. I am interested in Blacks resolving their identity crises and accepting their origin and heritage of Africa. I am interested in blacks tackling the worst political mismanagement of all times ravaging Africa, turning blacks into 'willing slaves' and destroying the black heritage.

History and historians tell us that the coming of Christopher Columbus in 1492 marked the beginning of Africa's humiliation globally and the loss of political autonomy, causing economic and social disruption.

But I have always contemplated these questions: How did Africa become a hunting ground for slaves? What was Africa's economic and political structure like before this time? What would have been the fate of all the slaves acquired by African kings and chiefs who were the real slave masters and dealers? They probably would have worked, lived and died in their chains and their descendants remain outcasts as it is still today in some African countries. These are called 'Osu' (outcast) those whose great grandparents were slaves in Igbo land, the Eastern part of Nigeria.

Till today, these set of people 'Osu' are not allowed to

marry a 'free-born' yet we accuse the Western world of discrimination and humiliation. In Dahomey (now Benin) which was one of the greatest slave regions in Africa, slaves were sacrificed and killed in an annual ceremony in their hundreds and thousands. Such was also the case in Cameron, where slaves were sacrificed for rituals annually.

What was the fate of twins and their mothers before the intervention of Mary Slessor? Twins were seen as evil and killed in Efik, an Eastern part of Nigeria, until the intervention of Mary Slessor, a Scottish missionary to Nigeria, born on 2 December 1848 in Aberdeen. She lived and devoted her time and life to the freedom of women and stopping the infanticide of twins until her death on 13 January 1915 at the age of sixty-six in Nigeria.

To date, the Western world, championed by the United Kingdom and America, are still fighting to rid Africa of the cruelty of female genital mutilation (FGM). Girls as young as twelve are still being forced into marriages. Are these the traditions, cultures and social heritage we should be proud of and accuse the Western world of distorting? I am sure the 21st century black African children are ashamed of such barbaric and uncivilized practices, culture and traditions. Little wonder they are ashamed to be called Africans.

We write and teach our children the history of slaves thrown overboard by slave masters. Slaves who were beaten to death and those who died in the plantations, without teaching them how slaves were sacrificed, killed, slaughtered in annual rituals in Africa and those still regarded as out-casts in some parts of Africa to date. Slavery has always existed in Africa. That was how Africa became a hunting ground.

Yes, the colonial masters were responsible for part of the troubles, disunity and religious crises in Africa by ignorantly mapping people of diverse culture, history and religious beliefs into a common colony, but I ask, have we not come of age enough to correct these things? Do we have leaders who understand the language of dialogue and referendum? Are we waiting for the colonial masters to return to correct these things? Kingdoms rise, kingdoms fall. Africa fell but has refused to rise.

More than 1 million Europeans were captured and sold as slaves in North Africa by Barbary Pirates between the 16th and 19th centuries.

In 1492, Europe began taking over America which they (Europeans) simply called the "New World" with the arrival of Spanish explorer, Christopher Columbus on December 5, 1492. Hence, Spain began the colonization of America followed by England in 1498 with the arrival of John Cabot. France and Portugal, all came in. America was taken over and colonized. Obviously, the colonization of America by Europe brought dramatic widespread changes to its landscape, culture, population, plant and animal life. This was known as Columbian exchange. They suffered communicable diseases and were taking as slaves.

Following the arrival of Europeans, the indigenous people of America suffered epidemics of smallpox, typhus, influenza, measles and diphtheria. Between 10 million and 100 million Americans died upon contact with Europeans. Europeans were then known to carry these germs as a result of living in close quarters with their domesticated animals. How much more destruction and distortion can a people go through, yet America rose to become the most powerful nation on planet Earth that even their former colonial masters now look up to them.

Africa had 'Nature's army' (mosquitoes) fighting for her. Malaria killed most of the first Europeans who came to Africa hence Africans were not infected with 'European germs' and did not suffer too many losses through communicable diseases like America. But we are the ones moaning the most, still counting losses and making excuses for our inability to govern ourselves and move forward. Blaming the whole world but ourselves.

Throughout the world and throughout history, nations

rise, and nations fall. Africa fell but has refused to rise. Instead, it chose the blame game and self-pity over productivity and good governance. America was colonized. Britain was conquered.

Perhaps, we should look at a nation like Great Britain. In 9 A.D, Britain lost three legions in the battle of the Teutoburg Forest in the hands of rebellious German tribesmen. They were completely destroyed. Decades later, in 43 A.D, Britain (Celtic as it was known then), was conquered and taken by Rome under Emperor Claudius after two failed attempts by Julius Caesar in 55 BC and 54 BC respectively.

For 400 years, Britain was under the rulership of Rome. It is worthy of note that millions suffered slavery under Roman rule. Their land – mineral resources like gold, silver, iron, zinc, etc – were exploited by the Romans. Their culture was eroded. They became Romanized.

Unlike Africa, Britain did not dwell on the wickedness, slavery and all the negative effects and consequences of Roman invasion. They were quick to acknowledge the positive impacts, and taught generations the same. They acknowledged that Romans gave them language, taught them how to build good roads and bridges and concretes. They gave them law, town planning and public architecture. In other words, the Romans brought them civilization (Romanization).

Britain, before the Roman invasion, was like Africa before the Colonial Era. It was then known as Celtic, had no central government, but it had chiefs. Their warriors were known for painting their faces blue. But unlike Africa, the Roman invasion and colonization transformed Britain into what it is today hence, Great Britain.

Haven learnt governance they became united and formed a central government. Instead of stirring up sentiments and resentment, they continued and built on the structure that the Roman Empire left behind. These, in no small way, opened doors of trade between Rome and Britain. International trade, as we all know, is at the centre of any nation's great economy.

About twelve million African slaves were taken to the Caribbean Islands, Mexico, Brazil and the Americas (United States) between the years 1619 and 1865. Their descendants are no longer Africans, but 'Black Americans' hence, have become willing slaves.

While we blame African tribal chiefs for their involvement in the slave trade, it is important to understand that African chiefs were not the only ones involved in domestic slavery. Neither was Africa the only continent associated with slave practices. In the Americas, slavery was practiced, including human sacrifice, before the arrival of the Europeans. It is therefore irrelevant to dwell on blame and demand apologies and compensation. Slavery and the slave trade was part of human civilization and development. Human civilization and development is a process.

In this 21st century, human rights and freedom of speech is still an issue in most countries. Gender equality is still being fought for. The world is still battling to eradicate what we know today as modern-day slavery. Human trafficking is still going on. I do not think that this generation of Britons know anything about Roman conquest and 400 years of occupancy, rule and exploitation of England by the Romans, except perhaps, students of history. Those who do, only know the positive impacts of Roman conquest and what the Romans brought and thought them. The name Britain came from the Roman goddess – Britannia.

The world has moved on. Why has Africa refused to move on? Britain was ruled by chiefs, had no central government, neither were they united prior to Roman conquest. But unlike Africa, England was united by this conquest hence, uniting and forming a central government upon independence. America became the United States of America and has gone further to becoming greater than their colonialists.

These days, we hear rumours of evil scientific

engineering going on in some parts of the Western world to exterminate the Black race and wipe them out from the surface of the earth through drugs, medicine, vaccines, poisonous food and water, including deadly viruses targeting the Black race. We hear of the so-called militants in Africa being sponsored and used by some Western governments and some Jewish merchants who own and control Africa's mineral resources like oil and diamonds.

Whether these rumours are true or not, there is a continent called Africa. That is the continent for the Black race but she has been abandoned by her own children. Where are the descendants of the twelve million blacks sold into slavery? We are no longer Africans; we now belong to other races. Why must the black race depend on other continents and races for survival? Despite having great black scientists and doctors, why must the black race depend on other races for medicine, food, science and technology?

Isn't it about time we shifted from the Joseph generation (slave generation) to Moses generation (leader's generation) to begin to lead the Black continent and the Black race-Africa? If Africa is developing her medicine, will African children and indeed black children, pregnant women, young women and men not be saved from evil scientific engineering, and any attempt to exterminate the black race?

We are told that the automatic gear system, automatic safety break system, the horizontally swinging barber's chair and the beer keg tap were all invented and developed by an African – Richard Bowie Spikes.

Alexander Miles was an African who invented the automatic opening and closing mechanism of an elevator door.

The cooling units in our cooling vans today that preserve perishable goods, ice blocks and ice cubes during transportation were invented by another African named Frederick McKinley Jones.

The modern-day letter box was invented by Philip B.

Downing. A black man.

The lantern we use, that is still being used in most homes worldwide was invented by another African called Michael C. Harvey.

Talk about African inventors like Garrett Morgan who, through his invention of the gas mask, saved group of workers trapped in a water intake tunnel 50 feet below Lake Erie in 1916. He also improved the functionality of the traffic light in America.

Granville T. Woods, born on Aril 23, 1856 and died on January 30, 1910, patented the communications between trains in transit and train stations in 1885. The egg incubator was also invented by this man, popularly referred to in his life time as 'black-Edison'. He was an African.

The history of man in space and how that mission was accomplished has always been told with no mention of the real brains behind it, the three brilliant African female mathematicians –Dorothy Vaughan, Katherine G. Johnson and Mary Jackson. This was showcased in the movie- *Hidden Figures*.

The pacemaker, a device that is implanted in the body to help regulate the heartbeat that saves millions of lives today daily was improved upon by an African called Otis Boykin.

We know of great Caucasian inventors like Bill Gates, Steve Jobs, Michael Dell (Dell computers), but how much do we as blacks know of the likes of Dr. Philip Emeagwali, a Nigerian who invented the world's fastest computer through his research of Honeycomb? In 1989, not too long ago, he used 65,000 processors to invent the world's fasted computer, which performs computations at 3.1 billion calculations per second. His computer is what is used in the weather forecast and in the prediction of global warming. An African. Just to mention a few.

It is therefore heartbreaking and disappointing that all this work and inventions were done in foreign lands. Think of what Africa would be if they were done in Africa? Africa's problem is not human resources; Africa's biggest problem is leadership drought. Africa has been left for too long in the hands of unqualified 'leaders' yet we are still concerned with protests to be recognized and accepted in the Western world rather than becoming leaders of Africa.

According to Deloitte Tourism, tourism accounted for 9.6% of total UK jobs in 2013, representing 3.1 million jobs. In 2013, tourism generated a total revenue of £126.9bn, representing 9% of UK GDP. In the United Kingdom, tourism has been a major job creator and is growing significantly more than sectors such as manufacturing, retail, construction, etc. Between 2010 and 2012 173,000 jobs were created within UK's tourism industry, at an average 4.7% per annum.

Tourism is the fastest growing sector in UK in employment terms, according to VisitBritain, with a forecast of over £257 billion worth of tourism industry by 2025, accounting for 9.9% of UK GDP. Supporting almost 3.8 million jobs, which is around 11% of the total UK population. The value of visitors entering the UK is expected to grow from over £21 billion in 2013 to £57 billion by 2025. In 2016, 37.6 million tourists visited the UK spending over £22.5 billion

This statistic shows data on international tourism revenue in Central America from 2005 to 2016. The region's tourism revenue amounted to USD 12.23 million in 2016, up from 11.35 million a year earlier (sttista.com). The U.S. travel and tourism industry contributed nearly USD 1.6 trillion to the U.S. economy in 2015 or 2.6 percent of its GDP. Travel and tourism exports accounted for 11 percent of all U.S. exports and 33 percent of all U.S. services exports, positioning travel and tourism as the nation's largest services export.

As expected, in the United States, the travel and tourism industry is one of the largest industries. In 2015, travel and tourism contributed USD 1.5 trillion to America's GDP. The industry is aiming towards contributing more than USD 2.6 trillion by 2027. Regarding employment, the travel and tourism industry in United States provides 5.5 million jobs directly annually.

Why is Africa still poor?

In the 1960s, Asia and Africa were on almost the same income levels but Asia has since over taken and outpaced Africa. It is true that there is corruption everywhere, but Asia's superior economic development lies in local investment. In contrast, African leaders use Swiss accounts to dump their loots, leaving the African nations in poverty and underdeveloped. Some of these loots exceed the total of their nations' external depts. Yet we sit back and watch. Yet we are leaders in the Western world.

Due to sustainable economic growth, China's tourism industry has seen unprecedented development and boom in recent years. In fact, the World Tourism Organisation predicts that China will become the largest travel destination and the fourth largest source country by 2020, predicting 137.10 international travellers by the year 2020, taking up 8.6% of the global share, and 100 million outbound Chinese visitors, 6.2% of the worldwide outbound visitors (China National Tourism Administration).

Despite being one of the leading luxury destinations worldwide and experiencing a growth of 59% in 2016, Kenya is still among the poorest nations of the world with a population of about 50,725,557 as of April 2018 according to Worldometers. Nearly half of Kenya's population live below the poverty line and are unable to meet the required daily nutrition (ruralpovertyportal.org).

Kenya's exports include agricultural products such as coffee, tea, fruit, vegetables and fresh flowers. Kenya has the second world's largest source of soda. It also boast deposits of gold and precious stones. Limestone and salt are also part of Kenya's main export products. Kenya is a major exporter of petroleum products from imported crude oil. Why then is half of the population living below poverty level and unemployment high? Political instability, corruption and bad governance – as in all African nations – have been the reasons for the poverty of the black race (our-africa.org). Natural tourism products and destinations abound in African

Tourism is one of the fastest growing industries worldwide and has a 100% growth rate of overall market share, a force to reckon with in terms of job creation and employment. The travel and tourism industry leads to massive billion-dollar revenues, with a high profitability rate around the globe. How is it that Africa, despite being blessed with human, mineral and natural resources, cannot profit by its tourism potentials? Can it not boost its economy? Can it not create jobs and employment? Can it not develop its infrastructure? Can it not control foreign exchange? Can it not protect its environment, make it clean and safe?

All the various nations of Africa need leadership that can build Africa's image; a leadership that will stamp out corruption and build internal security and develop infrastructure. Infrastructure is one of the factors that makes a destination attractive; a great boost for commerce and tourism. Hence, leadership that must ensure that infrastructural development is at the peak of their budget. Competitive high-tech architectural designs and structures are taking the centre stage globally. Modern airports, roads, railways and seaports, energy supplies, internet and adequate provision for healthcare must be up and running in Africa. A leadership that will focus on economic development and the creation of jobs. A leadership that will maximise the huge untapped natural tourism resources, potentials and products in Africa to sell Africa to the world, which will in turn boost her economy and elevate the suffering of the poor which unfortunately, is in the majority. A leadership that will make sound policies on foreign exchange, taxation, health care, education, security and infrastructural development. Africa cannot talk about or harness tourism potentials without sustainable and stable political structure. How can a continent whose leaders go abroad for medical treatment attract tourists? How can a continent ridden with corruption attract investors?

My background is African. Nigeria to be precise. It is a common fact that Africa is poor compared to the Western world, yet blessed with sunshine, mineral resources, nature, sandy beaches and good weather. I remember growing up in Nigeria as a young musician. The then-popular Lekki Beach in Lagos was the home of the biggest music festival referred to as Lekki Sun Splash, where both tourists and locals would do nothing for three days at a stretch, other than dance to the rhythm of the loud music from different artistes both local and foreign, against the rhythm of the waves of the sea on the gentle caressing hot sand during the day and the gentle sweet breeze of the ocean by night. Then they would rest and sleep under coconut trees while refreshing themselves with coconut water. Natural tourism products and destinations abound in Africa. Africa's weak economy can be a catalyst for booming tourism only if the issue of infrastructural development, political stability, security and health care is taken more seriously. All these are characteristics of unqualified leadership and leaders.

Nigeria, according to the World Bank *(2013)*, has a population of 173.6 million. In 2016, Nigeria's population stood at 186 million. In April 2018, according to Worldometer, Nigeria's population stands at 194, 934,273. This is equivalent to 2.57% of the total world population. It is arguably the most populous nation in Africa with over seventy world-class tourist destinations. It is known for its wildlife reserves and natural landmarks. Safari destinations such as Cross River National Park and waterfalls make Yankari National Park a must-see. The Zuma Rock, Coconut Beach, Bar Beach and Kainji National Park are just a few worth mentioning (*Nigerian Tourism Board*). It is therefore disheartening and sad to see that such a big nation, blessed with both human and natural resources, is not living to her full tourism potentials hence, high migration rate and fatalities across deserts and the Mediterranean Sea. Around 10.5 million children are out of school in Nigeria. Unemployment rate has doubled since 2015 causing the high surge in migration.

On November 5, 2016, twelve Nigerian women drowned trying to cross the Mediterranean Sea and were buried in Italy on November 17 of the same year with no Nigerian official in attendance. This is just one of many terrific and horrible cases.

Twenty-six Nigerian women migrants drowned in the Mediterranean in 2017 (Quartz Africa)

Each year, hundreds of thousands of Africans try to cross the deadly Mediterranean into Europe in search of 'greener pastures'. That is, if they are lucky enough to make it through a 1,300 mile drive across the Sahara Desert to Libya. This is where the journey of most African migrants ends. Most migrants attempt making this journey across the desert on foot. Some are raped and killed. Some are captured by militia groups who force them into marriages or use them for ransom. Some left at the mercies of human traffickers who auction and sell them in open slave markets, as seen in a recent CNN video report. In 2017 a staggering 160,000 African migrants attempted this deadly Mediterranean crossing. Over 3,000 died and many were unaccounted for. Women and girls who made it across, especially into Italy, simply became sex slaves. Children are separated from their parents. Yet we sit here and watch. Yet we still sing black and proud. Yet we have black leaders in the Western world who still do not see the need to think of leading Africa.

Dead bodies of African Migrants drowned in the sea.

We as blacks should take responsibility for any black life lost. We should take responsibility for any racial discrimination and abuse against any black child or children in Western schools and environments.

We petition the ill treatment and non-acceptance of migrants in Europe through Amnesty International, but how much do we petition and protest against African leaders who are responsible for the high volume of migrants fleeing hunger, starvation and bad leadership in Africa?

We sit back and watch African children pick food from the bins and refuse dumps. Drink water from the same ponds as animals. Black children forced to do manual labour as though they were slaves, with no home and shelter. Why would it take charity organisations to give ordinary water to African children? Why would it take charity organisations to give food to African children? Why would it take Europe to send relief materials and medicine to African children?

Make no mistake, Africa has great innovations and innovators, inventors, entrepreneurs. It has great human resources, patriots and investors. But we know that the structure, which is governance that is supposed to harness and create an enabling environment for development, is corrupt and unqualified.

How can you explain a culture where nothing is done or achieved by merit? According to a certain John, a foreigner who lived and worked in Africa for a good number of years. In his words concerning Nigeria which is a true reflation of all African nations.

He said:

"Everything is wrong with Nigeria. The director won't give you contract except you pay up front.

The banks won't give you loans except you concede a certain percentage.

The man supervising the contract won't pass the job unless you play ball.

The Clark won't pass your file for payment unless you "rub" his palm (bribe) him.

The accounts department won't raise your payment voucher or cheque unless you see (bribe) them."

These, John observed, as a common norm. And no one sees anything wrong with it. Is this the system that can produce quality leaders and leadership? I doubt.

He went on:

"Everything revolves around corruption. Nobody cares about anyone. No law and order.

Everybody is only desperate for one thing "money".

They will kill anyone and everything that stand in between them and money.

Highly skilled jobs and contracts are given to friends and relatives, to party members and fellow religious members who do not possess any basic skills or qualifications in those jobs."

John cannot figure out how he can convince his kids or any African child that education and hard work is rewarding.

He continued:

"When fools and touts are running the country from the local government to the presidency.

African leaders are corrupt, morally bankrupt and selfish. They only think about themselves and no one else."

John believes that only revolution by indigenous citizens who are feeling the pain can change the system.

This is where I beg to differ a bit.

Those who are feeling the pain are hungry and will do anything for a piece of bread, including singing praises and supporting those who have kept them in poverty. African leaders use poverty and illiteracy to hold citizens under their wicked control. Those who will lead the revolutions or promising change are still part of this corrupt culture. Quoting John's observation: "Corruption is a common norm, an acceptable way of life." Hence, I do not see any individual making any meaningful change.

African leadership needs a total wipe-out; a total overhauling, from bottom to top. A generation of leaders who are not part of this corrupt system, culture and nature. This is where blacks in the Western word come in, I believe.

But as long as we sit back in the Western world, denying our African heritage, refusing to acknowledge that we are from Africa and owe it to Africa to save Africa and indeed, the black race, with our knowledge of true and quality governance and leadership, and save Africa from the monopoly of unqualified leaders, no black anywhere in the world will have respect. Black children in the Western world will continue to be humiliated, irrespective of their personal achievements. "The darkest thing about Africa is our ignorance of it" - George Kimble.

*"DONALD TRUMP'S SPEECH ON WHY HE HATES AFRICANS & ARABS". *

*We are not obliged, even for a second, to try to prove to anybody and specially to blacks and Arabs that we are superior people - we have demonstrated that to the black and Arabs in 1001 ways. *

*The America we know today was not created by wishful thinking. We created it at the expenses of intelligence, sweat, and blood... we do not pretend like other whites that we like the blacks - We must admit, without any fear, that we don't like them, and for so, so, many valid reasons. *

*The fact that blacks and Arabs look like human beings does not necessarily make them sensible human beings. Hedgehogs are not porcupines and lizards are not crocodiles because they look alike. If God had wanted us to be equal to blacks and Arabs, he would have created us all of a uniform colour and intellect. But he created us differently. Whites, blacks, yellow, the rulers and the ruled. Intellectually we are superior to the blacks and Arabs. That has been proven beyond the reasonable doubt over the years. *

*I believe that a white man is an honest, God fearing person who has demonstrated practically the right way of being a human. By now every one of us has seen it practically that blacks and Arabs cannot rule themselves. Give them guns and they will kill each other. *

*They are good in nothing else but making noise, dancing, marrying many wives, alcoholism, witchcraft, indulging in sex, pretending in church, jealousy, fighting and complaining of bad leadership; but, yet refuse to take a decisive action and protest to remove the brigands from position of power. *

*Their only main concern (which according to me is stupidity of the highest magnitude) is same - sex marriages. They keep pointing fingers to us, we the west, that we have legalised it in our countries, and that we always outspokenly support gay people around the world. And because they always foolishly want to demonstrate their ignorance, hatred and fear about the subject, some of them have even enacted harsh laws to condemn their own gay citizens. This shows that beyond illusions and doubt, what people do with their own bodies is Africans main concern. I hear they even strip their women publicly. *

*Let us all accept the fact that the black man is a symbol of poverty, mental inferiority, laziness and emotional incompetence. To make the matter worse, he can do everything possible to defend his stupidity. Give them money for development and they will fight and create hatred and enmity for themselves. Drill oil wells for them and they will not have peace all the days of their life. *

*See, for instance, what's happening in Nigeria (a Country blessed with abundant resources), Southern Sudan, Malawi, DRC just to mention a few. *

"This proves to anybody including a stupid fool that Africans do not know what they want. isn't that plausible"?

*"They are like monkeys looking for already ripping banana all over the world! *

*Therefore, that the white man is created to rule the black man, Africans will always have day dreams. *

And here is the creature (black man) that lacks foresight but only sees what is near him and still fails to know what to do"

*A black man is stupid to the extent that he cannot plan for his life beyond a year. Therefore, how can they develop and live longer. *

*"Corruption in the west (And China) is a big

abomination, but in Africa, it's so huge that it is slowly becoming an acceptable way of life! *(Shame isn't it?)

They sing and rejoice to their corrupt political leaders. They worship their scandal-ridden religious leaders like their gods. Lest you forget, these so-called Africans are praising, dancing and praying for the people that have impoverished them, and who comes to hide their loot here.

*Then which fool argues that the black man is not born a beggar, grows a beggar, looks a beggar, falls sick as a beggar and dies a beggar. This has been proven beyond reasoning. *

*I wonder why even up to now most Africans still go to school by force, and those who are at school are just drug addicts who don't know what took them there. This is a pregnant stupidity in Africa that needs Jesus's immediate second coming. The body of Africans is a very fertile ground for all diseases in the world because they don't fear even HIV/AIDS. *

*This leaves me with a question: Are our eyes created the same with those Africans? I hear there are still cultures in Africa that prohibit them from using latrines which is very annoying. *

*"They cried for independence but have failed to rule themselves". For sure being African is a very untreatable disease that even prayers are not enough. *

*They have minerals, but they cannot do anything with it. Therefore, let us (whites) go to Africa and pick what we can pick and leave what is of no use. Poverty is a disease to the whites, but to the blacks it is very normal. *

*"Look at what is currently going on in Nigeria National Assembly. Legislators amending the constitution to favour themselves at the expense of two (200) million Nigerians. The present administration now has no economic blueprint

plan, rather than noise and false propaganda. Characterised with hatred and witch hunt/impoverishment". *

*"Majority of these legislators are treasury looters who are intellectually barren but using the ill-gotten wealth to oppress the citizens of that great country". *

*"What a shame"! *

*Black people with black sense, and a sick president in London for medical tourism! *

*The worst tragedy in Africa is that if you dare stand up and speak up for what's right, you may end up regretting.

*"The few wise and open-minded Africans who have tried to educate these fools about civilization have met the worst. They have been pushed hard on the wall, they have been silenced and others have been killed".

*Before I finish, let me tell Africans that before you jump and call me a racist, an anti-blacks or whatever term you may wish to use against me, 1st tackle runaway corruption, dreadful terrorism, tribalism, poverty, unemployment, diseases, illiteracy, ignorance, and inequality, that have put your whole continent on the verge of collapse".

*"Hate me or love me, I don't care. I know this is the plain truth which will never see the light of the day to the cowards that are afraid to be told as it is". *

*"Jesus please hurry and save Africans and Arabs".

*By- Donald J. Trump.

Tribute#RISEUPAFRICA!

Trump may be ignorant. He may even be insane. As childish as some of his comments may be, he's not altogether stupid. Is there not a cause? Is there not a reason? Is there no truth in most of the things he said? To dismiss some of these facts with a wave of hand is to deceive ourselves. We don't need people like Trump to tell us the hard truth. The truth is staring us in the face. Time has come for the bitter truth to be told. Our cry against discrimination and inequality against blacks is only for our convenience. The discrimination against blacks in the Western world is nothing compared to the discrimination and abandonment of Africa by blacks. I do respect all black political and public office holders in the Western world; that shows we have what it takes to lead, rule and govern. But I do not respect the fact that we do not see ourselves as Africans and have abandoned Africa and cannot govern Africa.

Trump knows that most of the so-called American inventions were done and still been done by blacks. Do you blame him? All these inventions done in America and all credit given to America. If blacks in the Western world deny Africa freedom, then we don't deserve it ourselves. "Those who deny freedom to others deserve it not for themselves"- Abraham Lincoln.

"You may choose to look the other way, but you can never say again that you did not know"

- William Wilberforce.

"Give me six hours to chop down a tree and I will use the first four hours sharpening the axe"- Lincoln.

This is a reality check and call to all Igbo's home and abroad, especially those clamouring for the Republic of Biafra.

I watch with mixed feelings, sadness and joy when I see able-bodied educated young men and women from the Igbo tribe of Nigeria take to the streets of America and Europe with passion, chanting and clamouring for secession from Nigeria, clamouring for war. So sad to know that the only solution to Africa's problem these educated Africans can think of, even in this 21st century, is war and secession. Yet my heart is filled with joy seeing their passion and commitment to what they believe in.

What I see is a generation of change. Change, not by war or secession but by ballot. "The power of ballot is stronger than the power of bullet"- Abraham Lincoln.

I see educated young men and women who can make a difference, make a change as senators, governors, ministers, local government chair persons. I see a generation who live in the Western world and understand that corruption has no place in modern-day society. Who understands that education holds the key to any healthy nation and economy. A generation who understands the dynamics of wealth creation and development.

The principle of tribal secession and war with all the misery it brings especially to children must be discouraged in its entirety.

Yes, all the signs that led to 1967 Nigerian Civil War are still present.

Yes, we know the Northerners are killing the Igbos (Easterners).

Yes, we know there's monopoly of power by the North.

Yes, we know resources are not equitably distributed.

But you cannot do things the same way and expect different results.

I will forever respect Chief Emeka Odimegwu Ojukwu, who led the 'Biafran' soldiers. He did what he had to do as a young soldier and according to the level of civilization then. Nigeria and indeed, Africa did not have a strong political structure then and was ruled mainly by the military. Less we forget, the military was in power under General Yakubu Gowan. So, it was the Northern soldiers against the Eastern soldiers.

Fifty years on and counting, we cannot be talking tribal war and secession. Nigeria should be a leading civilized nation in Africa.

Sadly enough, well-educated Igbos living in the civilized Western world are engulfed in this ignorance. Raising Biafran flags, wearing Biafran T-shirts and singing Nzogbu-Nzogbu (war song) in the streets of America, Britain and all over Europe.

For those who did not know, over 1 million people died in just two and half years of civil war in Nigeria. Men, women and children, thousands died from hunger and starvation. Both civilians and soldiers. Men and soldiers were being shot and killed in the presence of their wives and children.

My uncle, a soldier who tried to hide under my father's bed, was shot at point blank in our room at Ibadan where it all began, by the Northern soldiers in the presence of my mother and my two elder brothers who were only kids then. His brains and blood covered the whole room as he was shot in the head and his body was left with my mum and her two infant children. My father was shot in the chest as he jumped through the window of a second floor army barracks building. Thank God he survived to tell us the real story. How many lived to tell the story?

I was born in the forest, left at the mercy of cold, soldier ants, snakes and wild animals while my father was in the battle field fighting for Biafra.

The big question is what have Igbo leaders and governors done with the 'little' federal allocation (money) given to the States and local councils monthly?

What have they done with the abundant human, mineral and natural resources God has blessed Igbo land with?

I make bold to say that the same 'unfair' distribution of federal resources was still present when a visionary leader, Dr Sam Onulaka Mbakwe developed the then Imo state, built schools, hospitals and roads. Built industries and created jobs.

Who are the Igbo leaders to be trusted? Do we still have visionary leaders? I suppose not.

Greatness, recognition and respect as a people can only come through education, economic empowerment and liberation. Sadly, Igbo leaders are only interested in personal wealth creation.

Not making excuses for the rumoured importation of weapons by the North, but I do not know of any government who will sit back and watch a tribe openly parading a nation inside a nation.

I will therefore plead with radio Biafra to use their media to hold Igbo leaders and governors accountable rather than instigate or cause division and hatred among tribes.

The Rwandan genocide of 1994 that saw almost 1.2

million dead in just one hundred days started with a radio station created for same purpose.

There are still unanswered questions on why the Igbos lost the Civil War:

- The position and role of the Niger Delta.
- The greed, mistrust and betrayal among Igbo leaders.
- The role of the Western world.

I do not want to mention names, but just like Ojukwu, it was not the Northerners that stopped Dr Ekwueme from contesting the presidency in the Second Republic, it was his fellow Igbo leaders like Jim Nwobodo and co. Please, Radio Biafra, do not act as another Rwandan radio Machete. Generation will not forgive us and all other propaganda media and campaigners if we allow dubious, corrupt, wicked individuals and countries who profit from the sale of weapons with no regard for human lives, especially children, or in exchange for Africa's mineral resources, to use you.

If Britain supported Nigerian forces against Biafra to protect their interest in Nigeria's oil by given them weapons, intelligence and mercenaries, they're not likely to change positions now.

If France, although calling the killing of Igbos genocide, sympathising with Biafra and supporting Biafra on the lip giving them outdated weapons but did not recognise Biafra as a nation while secretly selling weapons to Nigerian troops, they are likely to do same again.

If America stood aside and watched because Nigeria is in the British territory, the situation is not likely to change now.

War is not the hope and future we need for African youths and children. Education and job creation is the future and hope for African youths and children. There are educated young Africans who can make a change, who can make a difference, but do not have the opportunity because of the cabal of wicked unqualified leaders clinging to power and handing over leadership baton to their stooges as though it was a relay race. This is the battle we must fight and win. To break these powers that be and set Africa free. "The drums of Africa still beat in my heart. They will not let me rest while there is a single Nigro boy or girl without a chance to prove his worth" – Mary McLeod Bethune.

Sometimes I question our mental claim for superiority as black race. When all I see is a race with little or no mental power, willingness and passion to be proud of who they are, believe in who they are, identify with who they are and build who they are.

I see a race so divided, disunited and too weak and afraid to stand alone.

I see a race so crafty, so subtle, capitalizing on other races' weakness and goodwill to gain positions and places in already made structures, systems, establishments and societies.

I see a race that is not ashamed of using slavery and the slave era to blackmail other races.

I see a race that would blame the whole world for their misfortune just to cover up their weaknesses and inability to rule themselves.

I see a race locked up and imprisoned in their past, hence remaining willing slaves.

I see a race that has lost their identity, not knowing who they are; neither do their children know where they belong.

I see a race that will not admit their failures and weaknesses, neither would they recognise nor appreciate other races' efforts and contributions towards making them what they are.

What then is the solution to Africa's problem?

Blacks must know who they are, identify with their origins (Africa). What you are is not as important as who you are.

Blacks must unit and fight in a legal battle against any

African country, leader or constitution that do not allow dual citizenship, giving rights to blacks all over the world to vote and be voted for in the country of their ancestry. “None of us is as smart as all of us.” Unanimous

The solution to Africa’s problem is governance. By governance, I do not refer to the crop of leaders in Africa. Nothing good can ever come out of a corrupt system. “The world suffers a lot. Not because of the violence of bad people. But because of the silence of good people” – Napoleon.

Africa is suffering not because of the bad leaders but because Africa has been abandoned by those who are supposed to lead them.

Blacks in the Western world must rise and be prepared to take over the government of Africa by forming new generation political parties. “The power of ballot is stronger than the power of the bullet”- Abraham Lincoln.

“Regardless of what barriers confront you, it is in your power to free yourselves; you have only to want to”- Olympe de Gouges.

www.ingramcontent.com/pod-product-compliance
Ingram Content Group UK Ltd.
Pitfield, Milton Keynes, MK11 3LW, UK
UKHW021050270726
13967UKWH00012B/201

9 781789 552539